MASTERING
MICROSOFT
POWERPOINT 2024:

Unveiling the Advanced Features and Techniques of Microsoft PowerPoint

Gerard Stafford.

TABLE OF CONTENTS

CHAPTER ONE

INTRODUCTION

In the dynamic landscape of digital communication and business presentations, Microsoft PowerPoint remains a cornerstone tool for professionals and educators alike. This chapter serves as a gateway into the world of PowerPoint, offering an overview of its evolution, purpose, and the scope of the comprehensive guide aimed at unraveling its advanced features and techniques.

1.1 Overview of Microsoft PowerPoint

Microsoft PowerPoint, a part of the Microsoft Office suite, has come a long way since its inception. Originally introduced in 1987 as

"Presenter" for Macintosh, it has undergone numerous transformations, adapting to technological advancements and user needs. Today, it stands as a powerful presentation software used globally for creating visually compelling and impactful presentations.

The chapter opens with a brief historical overview, tracing the key milestones in PowerPoint's development. From its early days as a simple slideshow creator to its integration with cloud-based collaboration in recent versions, readers gain insight into the software's journey.

1.2 Evolution of PowerPoint

To understand the capabilities of PowerPoint 2024, it's crucial to appreciate the evolutionary steps that led to its current state. The evolution spans user interface improvements, feature enhancements, and the integration of multimedia elements. This section delves into the major updates and innovations that have shaped PowerPoint into a versatile tool for both novice and experienced users.

1.3 Purpose and Scope of the Guide

Why invest time in mastering PowerPoint? This section articulates the guide's purpose, emphasizing the value of acquiring advanced skills in PowerPoint for professional growth, effective communication, and streamlined collaboration. By setting clear expectations, readers can navigate the guide with a sense of purpose, understanding the practical benefits awaiting them.

1.4 How to Use This Book

To maximize the guide's utility, readers need guidance on how to navigate its content efficiently. This section provides an overview of the book's structure, explaining how each chapter builds upon the previous one. Additionally, it introduces the concept of hands-on exercises and practical examples, encouraging active learning and application of acquired knowledge.

As readers embark on their journey through the guide, they can expect a blend of theoretical concepts, step-by-step tutorials, and real-world scenarios. The goal is not only to impart knowledge but to empower users with the skills to confidently tackle diverse presentation challenges.

CHAPTER TWO

UNDERSTANDING THE BASICS

Having set the groundwork in Chapter 1, the subsequent chapters will delve into the practical aspects of PowerPoint. Chapter 2, titled "Understanding the Basics," is designed to ensure a solid foundation before venturing into advanced features. It covers fundamental aspects such as navigating the interface, creating and managing slides, inserting and formatting text, and working with images and graphics.

2.1 Navigating the PowerPoint Interface

The chapter kicks off with a detailed exploration of the PowerPoint interface.

Readers will become familiar with the ribbon, quick access toolbar, and various tabs. Understanding the layout and organization of the interface is pivotal for efficient use of the software. The chapter will also introduce customization options, allowing users to tailor the interface to suit their workflow.

2.2 Creating and Managing Slides

Building on interface familiarity, this section focuses on the core element of PowerPoint: slides. Readers will learn how to create, duplicate, and delete slides. Emphasis is placed on slide layouts, guiding users in selecting the most suitable layout for their content. The chapter will introduce strategies for organizing slides, managing sections, and utilizing the Slide Sorter view.

2.3 Inserting and Formatting Text

Text is a fundamental component of any presentation. This section provides a deep dive into inserting and formatting text within PowerPoint slides. From basic text boxes to advanced formatting options, users will gain proficiency in presenting textual information in a visually appealing manner. The discussion extends to text alignment, spacing, and the use of styles for consistency.

2.4 Working with Images and Graphics

Visual elements elevate presentations, making them more engaging and memorable.

This part of the chapter explores the insertion and manipulation of images and graphics. Topics include image formats, resizing and cropping, and integrating icons and shapes into slides. Readers will also discover techniques for aligning and grouping objects, enhancing the overall visual impact of their presentations.

Through a combination of theoretical explanations and hands-on exercises, Chapter 2 aims to equip users with a solid understanding of PowerPoint's fundamental features. The goal is to establish a robust foundation that will serve as a springboard for the advanced techniques explored in subsequent chapters. Readers are encouraged to actively engage with the software, applying the concepts learned and gaining confidence in their ability to navigate and manipulate PowerPoint's basic elements.

CHAPTER THREE

ADVANCED SLIDE DESIGN TECHNIQUES

With a solid grasp of the basics from Chapter 2, Chapter 3 takes a deep dive into advanced slide design techniques. This chapter is dedicated to empowering users with the skills to create visually stunning and professionally designed presentations.

3.1 Mastering Slide Layouts

Building upon the knowledge of basic slide creation, this section explores the intricacies of slide layouts. Readers will discover the power of customizing layouts to suit specific content and design preferences. Techniques for creating master slides and establishing a consistent design across multiple slides are unveiled, providing a foundation for cohesive and visually appealing presentations.

3.2 Customizing Themes and Colors

Themes and colors play a pivotal role in presentation aesthetics. In this segment, users will learn to go beyond default themes, unlocking the full potential of customization. The chapter covers selecting, creating, and modifying themes to align with branding or personal preferences. Additionally, it delves into color schemes, guiding users on creating harmonious and impactful color palettes.

3.3 Incorporating Multimedia Elements

Multimedia elements, such as audio and video, can significantly enhance a presentation's impact. This section provides step-by-step guidance on embedding and formatting multimedia elements within PowerPoint. From adding background music to integrating video clips, users will gain the skills to captivate their audience and convey information in a dynamic and engaging manner.

3.4 Animations and Transitions

The art of animation and transitions is explored in this part of the chapter. Users will understand how to breathe life into their presentations by incorporating subtle animations and smooth transitions between slides. The guide covers entrance, emphasis, and exit animations, along with advanced animation options for precise control over visual elements.

3.5 Tips for Consistent Design Across Slides

Consistency is key in professional presentations. This final section of Chapter 3 provides invaluable tips and best practices for maintaining a uniform design throughout a presentation. Topics include using slide masters, creating custom layouts, and leveraging design guides to ensure a polished and cohesive look across all slides.

CHAPTER FOUR

COLLABORATION AND SHARING

As we progress through the guide to mastering Microsoft PowerPoint 2024, Chapter 4 emerges as a pivotal exploration into the collaborative and sharing features embedded within the software. In an era defined by interconnectedness and remote collaboration, understanding how PowerPoint facilitates seamless teamwork is essential for professionals across various domains.

4.1 Collaborative Editing in PowerPoint

Collaborative editing is a hallmark feature of modern productivity tools, and PowerPoint is no exception. This section begins by introducing readers to the collaborative landscape of PowerPoint, where multiple users can work on a presentation simultaneously. The chapter navigates through real-time editing, highlighting features like comments, track changes, and version history. Users will discover the art of effective collaboration, whether working with colleagues in the same office or remotely across different time zones.

The exploration extends to tips for managing collaborative projects efficiently, ensuring smooth workflows and avoiding potential conflicts. Readers will gain insights into best practices for communication within the PowerPoint environment, fostering a collaborative spirit that enhances productivity and creativity.

4.2 Sharing Presentations Online

In an increasingly digital world, the ability to share presentations online is a game-changer. This section delves into the myriad ways users can share their PowerPoint creations with a broader audience. From basic sharing options to advanced features like password protection and access controls, readers will become adept at tailoring their sharing strategies based on the intended audience and purpose.

The chapter guides users through the process of creating shareable links, embedding presentations on websites, and utilizing cloud-based platforms for seamless sharing. Security considerations are also explored, ensuring that users can confidently distribute their presentations without compromising sensitive information.

4.3 Real-time Collaboration Features

Real-time collaboration goes beyond mere editing; it's a dynamic interaction that transforms the way teams work together. This part of the chapter zooms in on advanced real-time collaboration features, shedding light on functionalities like live chat, presence awareness, and co-authoring in PowerPoint. Users will learn how to leverage these features to enhance communication and streamline collaborative efforts.

The discussion extends to integrating PowerPoint with other collaboration tools, such as Microsoft Teams and SharePoint. By understanding the synergy between PowerPoint and these platforms, users can create a seamless collaborative environment, breaking down geographical barriers and fostering a sense of unity among team members.

4.4 Integrating with Microsoft 365

Microsoft 365 is the backbone of modern productivity, and this section explores how PowerPoint seamlessly integrates into this ecosystem. From accessing presentations on multiple devices to utilizing OneDrive for cloud storage, users will discover the full spectrum of Microsoft 365 integration. The chapter also covers the advantages of using Microsoft 365 for real-time collaboration, offering a comprehensive understanding of the interconnectedness of Microsoft's suite of tools.

Through practical examples and case studies, readers will grasp the strategic implications of Microsoft 365 integration, unlocking new possibilities for collaborative work. The chapter concludes by providing guidance on optimizing workflows, ensuring that users harness the full potential of PowerPoint within the broader Microsoft 365 ecosystem.

CHAPTER FIVE

DATA VISUALIZATION WITH POWERPOINT

In the ever-evolving landscape of business and education, effective data visualization is a crucial skill. Chapter 5 delves into the intricate world of data visualization with Microsoft PowerPoint 2024, empowering users to convey complex information in a visually compelling and easily understandable manner.

5.1 Creating Effective Charts and Graphs

The chapter commences with an exploration of PowerPoint's robust capabilities for creating various types of charts and graphs.

Readers will embark on a journey through the essentials of data-driven presentations, learning how to choose the right chart type based on the nature of the data. From bar charts to pie charts and beyond, this section offers a comprehensive guide to creating visually appealing and informative charts.

The discussion extends to advanced chart customization options, empowering users to tailor the appearance of charts to align with the presentation's overall design. Techniques such as adjusting axis scales, formatting data labels, and incorporating trendlines are unveiled, providing users with the tools to transform raw data into compelling visual narratives.

5.2 Data-Driven Presentations

Moving beyond static charts, this section introduces the concept of data-driven presentations. Users will discover how to link PowerPoint slides to external data sources, enabling dynamic updates as underlying data changes. This not only streamlines the process of updating presentations but also ensures accuracy and relevance in data representation.

Practical examples guide users through the process of creating data connections, whether pulling data from Excel spreadsheets, databases, or online sources. The chapter emphasizes the importance of maintaining data integrity and provides best practices for seamless integration of external data into PowerPoint presentations.

5.3 Advanced Chart Customization

Building on the foundation laid in the previous section, this part of the chapter delves into advanced chart customization techniques. Users will learn how to go beyond default settings, exploring features like 3D chart effects, color mapping, and interactive elements. The goal is to empower users with the skills to create visually stunning charts that captivate audiences and effectively convey complex data sets.

The chapter provides insights into leveraging PowerPoint's tools for fine-tuning chart elements, such as axes, legends, and data labels. Additionally, it explores the integration of multimedia elements within charts, offering users the ability to create dynamic and engaging data visualizations.

5.4 Incorporating Excel Data into PowerPoint

Microsoft Excel is a powerhouse for data analysis, and this section demonstrates how to seamlessly integrate Excel data into PowerPoint presentations. Users will discover the benefits of embedding Excel charts and tables directly into PowerPoint slides, ensuring data consistency and easy updates.

The chapter covers the process of creating and updating embedded Excel objects, enabling users to maintain a live connection between PowerPoint and Excel.

This integration not only enhances the efficiency of data management but also opens the door to collaborative workflows between Excel and PowerPoint users.

Through hands-on exercises and real-world examples, readers will gain practical experience in data visualization with PowerPoint.

CHAPTER SIX

MASTERING SMARTART AND 3D MODELS

In the dynamic landscape of modern presentations, visual elements play a pivotal role in conveying complex ideas with clarity and impact. Chapter 6 of "Mastering Microsoft PowerPoint 2024" takes a deep dive into the advanced features of SmartArt and 3D Models, empowering users to elevate their presentations to new heights of visual sophistication.

6.1 *Enhancing Visual Communication with SmartArt*

SmartArt, a feature embedded within Microsoft PowerPoint, transforms mundane lists and bullet points into visually appealing diagrams and graphics. This section begins by introducing readers to the diverse range of SmartArt graphics available, each tailored for specific types of information representation.

Readers will explore the step-by-step process of creating and customizing SmartArt graphics to effectively communicate complex ideas. From organizational charts to process diagrams, users will gain a comprehensive understanding of how SmartArt can enhance visual communication within their presentations.

6.2 Creating and Customizing 3D Models

The journey through Chapter 6 continues with an exploration of 3D models—an advanced feature that brings a new dimension to PowerPoint presentations. This section introduces readers to the intricacies of inserting and customizing 3D models within slides. From simple geometric shapes to intricate models, users will discover the versatility of 3D elements in enhancing visual appeal and engagement.

Practical examples guide users through the process of adjusting lighting, angles, and perspectives to achieve the desired visual impact. The chapter emphasizes the seamless integration of 3D models with other PowerPoint features, such as animations and transitions, enabling users to create immersive and dynamic presentations.

6.3 Integrating 3D Models into Presentations

Building on the foundation established in the previous section, this part of the chapter focuses on the strategic integration of 3D models into presentations. Users will learn how to strategically place and animate 3D models to convey information effectively. Whether showcasing product designs, architectural concepts, or molecular structures, readers will gain the skills to leverage 3D models as powerful visual aids.

The chapter explores best practices for maintaining a cohesive design when incorporating 3D elements and provides insights into optimizing performance for seamless presentations. Users will also discover the potential for interactivity, allowing audiences to engage with 3D models during presentations.

6.4 Advanced Tips for Visual Impact

As the chapter unfolds, it culminates with a collection of advanced tips aimed at maximizing visual impact. This section serves as a treasure trove of insights, covering topics such as creating cinematic transitions, utilizing morph transitions for seamless animations, and leveraging advanced formatting options.

Readers will gain proficiency in harnessing the full potential of SmartArt and 3D models to create presentations that captivate and resonate with their audience. The chapter emphasizes experimentation and creativity, encouraging users to explore unconventional approaches to visual storytelling within PowerPoint.

CHAPTER SEVEN

AUTOMATION AND MACROS IN POWERPOINT

In the ever-evolving landscape of productivity tools, automation has become a cornerstone for efficiency and precision. Chapter 7 of "Mastering Microsoft PowerPoint 2024" delves into the realm of automation and macros, unraveling the potential for streamlining tasks, enhancing workflows, and unlocking a new level of control within PowerPoint.

7.1 Introduction to Macros

The chapter kicks off with a comprehensive introduction to macros, demystifying the concept for users who might be new to automation within PowerPoint. Macros are sequences of instructions that automate repetitive tasks, and this section elucidates their role in enhancing productivity.

Readers will gain insights into the macro recorder, a tool that allows users to record a series of actions for later playback. The chapter navigates through the basics of creating and executing macros, providing a foundation for users to harness the power of automation within their PowerPoint workflows.

7.2 Creating and Using Macros

Building on the foundation laid in the introductory section, this part of the chapter delves deeper into the creation and utilization of macros. Users will learn how to write and edit VBA (Visual Basic for Applications) code, the programming language that underlies macros in PowerPoint.

Practical examples guide users through the process of creating macros to automate tasks such as formatting, slide creation, and repetitive edits. The chapter emphasizes the importance of understanding VBA syntax and structure, empowering users to customize and tailor macros to suit their specific needs.

7.3 Automation with Visual Basic for Applications (VBA)

Visual Basic for Applications (VBA) is the powerhouse behind macros, providing a versatile and powerful programming environment within PowerPoint. This section immerses users in the world of VBA, exploring its syntax, structure, and the multitude of functions and objects available.

Readers will gain proficiency in writing VBA code to automate complex tasks, such as creating interactive presentations, generating dynamic content, and performing data manipulations. The chapter guides users through the process of integrating VBA with PowerPoint's object model, unlocking a vast array of possibilities for customization and automation.

7.4 Enhancing Efficiency with Macros

As users progress through the chapter, the focus shifts to practical applications of macros for enhancing efficiency within PowerPoint. This part of the chapter provides a repertoire of real-world scenarios where macros can be deployed to save time and reduce manual effort.

From automating repetitive formatting tasks to creating custom tools for specific workflows, readers will discover the strategic advantages of incorporating macros into their PowerPoint toolkit. The chapter also explores best practices for organizing and managing macros, ensuring a streamlined and efficient automation process.

The chapter concludes with a reflection on the transformative potential of automation and macros within PowerPoint. Users are encouraged to explore and experiment with the newfound skills acquired, paving the way for a more efficient and dynamic approach to presentation creation and management.

Through hands-on exercises and guided tutorials, users will have the opportunity to apply the concepts learned in practical scenarios. By the end of Chapter 7, readers will emerge with a comprehensive understanding of automation and macros, ready to leverage these tools to enhance their productivity within PowerPoint.

CHAPTER EIGHT

TIPS FOR DYNAMIC PRESENTATIONS

In the ever-evolving landscape of presentations, captivating your audience and conveying information effectively are essential skills. Chapter 8 of "Mastering Microsoft PowerPoint 2024" delves into the art of dynamic presentations, exploring techniques, strategies, and tips to engage your audience and leave a lasting impression.

8.1 Engaging Your Audience Effectively

The chapter begins by emphasizing the importance of audience engagement. Effective presentations are not just about conveying information; they are about creating a connection with your audience. This section explores various methods to captivate your audience from the outset, including compelling introductions, storytelling techniques, and audience interaction strategies.

Readers will delve into the psychology of engagement, understanding how to tailor presentations to resonate with different audience types. From business professionals to educators, the chapter provides insights into crafting presentations that not only inform but also inspire and resonate with the target audience.

8.2 Effective Storytelling Techniques

Storytelling is a powerful tool that transcends industries and disciplines. This section delves into the art of effective storytelling within PowerPoint presentations. Readers will learn the elements of a compelling story, including character development, plot structure, and thematic coherence.

Practical examples guide users through the process of integrating storytelling techniques into their presentations, transforming dry data into a narrative that engages and resonates. The chapter also explores the use of visuals, anecdotes, and real-life examples to enhance storytelling and create a memorable impact.

8.3 Incorporating Interactive Elements

Interactivity is a key ingredient in maintaining audience interest and involvement. This part of the chapter introduces readers to various interactive elements that can be seamlessly incorporated into PowerPoint presentations. From clickable navigation to interactive quizzes and polls, users will discover how to make their presentations a two-way communication channel.

The chapter explores the integration of hyperlinks, action buttons, and navigation features, allowing users to create presentations that respond to audience input. Real-world examples showcase the effectiveness of interactive elements in different settings, from boardroom meetings to virtual webinars.

8.4 Handling Q&A Sessions

A well-prepared Q&A session can elevate a presentation from informative to interactive. This section provides guidance on effectively handling Q&A sessions, offering tips for anticipating and addressing questions with confidence and clarity.

Readers will gain insights into creating a conducive environment for questions, managing time effectively, and addressing challenging queries. The chapter also explores strategies for encouraging audience participation and feedback, fostering a collaborative atmosphere that extends beyond the presentation itself.

8.5 Tips for Consistent Design Across Slides

Consistency in design is a hallmark of professional presentations. This part of the chapter revisits the concept of consistent design, providing additional tips and best practices. Users will explore advanced techniques for maintaining visual cohesion across slides, including the use of design templates, color palettes, and font consistency.

The chapter also addresses the importance of accessibility in design, ensuring that presentations are inclusive and accessible to diverse audiences. Techniques for creating presentations that are visually appealing and user-friendly for individuals with varying abilities are discussed, aligning with modern standards of inclusivity in design.

8.6 Adapting to Different Presentation Environments

Presentations can take place in diverse environments, from traditional boardrooms to virtual settings. This section guides users on adapting their presentation style to different environments. Readers will gain insights into tailoring content, adjusting delivery methods, and utilizing technology effectively based on the presentation setting.

The chapter explores strategies for virtual presentations, addressing challenges such as maintaining engagement in online environments and leveraging collaboration tools for effective communication. Whether presenting to a small team in person or a global audience via video conferencing, users will learn to navigate and excel in various presentation contexts.

8.7 Leveraging Advanced Animation Techniques

Animation, when used judiciously, can enhance the visual appeal and effectiveness of presentations. This part of the chapter delves into advanced animation techniques, providing users with the skills to create sophisticated and polished animations that complement their content.

From entrance and exit animations to motion paths and custom animations, readers will explore the diverse range of animation options within PowerPoint. The chapter also provides guidance on using animation to convey information dynamically, ensuring that each animation serves a purpose in enhancing the audience's understanding.

8.8 Navigating Presentation Challenges

The final section of the chapter addresses common presentation challenges and provides strategic solutions. From technical glitches to unexpected questions, readers will gain insights into navigating challenges with poise and professionalism. Real-world scenarios and case studies showcase how effective strategies can turn potential pitfalls into opportunities for growth and improvement.

The chapter concludes with a reflection on the holistic approach to dynamic presentations. Users are encouraged to view presentations as dynamic, evolving experiences rather than static slideshows. By incorporating storytelling, interactivity, and adaptability, presenters can create an engaging and memorable experience for their audience.

Through a combination of theoretical discussions, practical examples, and hands-on exercises, users will have the opportunity to hone their skills in crafting dynamic presentations. By the end of Chapter 8, readers will possess a comprehensive toolkit for creating presentations that not only convey information but also captivate, engage, and leave a lasting impact on their audience.

CHAPTER NINE

TROUBLESHOOTING AND OPTIMIZATION

In the realm of technology and software, challenges and unexpected issues can arise. Chapter 9 of "Mastering Microsoft PowerPoint 2024" addresses the crucial aspects of troubleshooting and optimization. Understanding how to navigate common problems and optimize the performance of PowerPoint ensures a seamless and efficient presentation experience.

9.1 Common Issues and Solutions

This section begins by identifying and addressing common issues that users may encounter while working with PowerPoint. From formatting glitches to compatibility problems, readers will explore practical solutions and troubleshooting techniques. The chapter emphasizes the importance of proactive problem-solving, empowering users to address challenges swiftly and effectively.

Real-world scenarios and case studies provide insights into diagnosing and resolving issues, ensuring that users are well-prepared to handle unexpected situations during presentations. The goal is to instill confidence in users, enabling them to troubleshoot common problems independently.

9.2 Optimizing Performance

Optimizing the performance of PowerPoint is essential for a smooth and efficient user experience. This part of the chapter delves into strategies for enhancing the performance of PowerPoint presentations, ensuring that they run seamlessly on different devices and platforms.

Readers will explore techniques for reducing file sizes, optimizing multimedia elements, and streamlining animations. The chapter also addresses considerations for presentations in online and offline modes, providing users with the knowledge to adapt their presentations to varying circumstances without sacrificing quality.

9.3 Security Best Practices

Security is a paramount concern, especially when dealing with sensitive information in presentations. This section guides users through best practices for securing PowerPoint presentations. Topics include password protection, encryption, and strategies for safeguarding confidential data.

The chapter explores features such as Information Rights Management (IRM) that enhance the security of PowerPoint files. Users will gain insights into mitigating risks associated with sharing presentations and learn how to implement security measures that align with organizational policies and standards.

9.4 Regular Updates and Maintenance

Staying up-to-date with software updates and performing regular maintenance is crucial for optimal performance. This part of the chapter introduces users to the importance of staying current with PowerPoint updates and provides guidance on how to manage updates effectively.

Readers will learn about new features, bug fixes, and security patches introduced through updates. The chapter also covers best practices for maintaining a clean and organized presentation environment, including file management strategies and the use of backup solutions to prevent data loss.

9.5 Accessibility Considerations

Accessibility is an integral aspect of creating inclusive presentations. This section focuses on considerations and best practices for ensuring that PowerPoint presentations are accessible to individuals with diverse abilities. Readers will explore features such as alt text, accessible design principles, and compatibility with screen readers.

The chapter emphasizes the importance of designing presentations that cater to a wide audience, including individuals with visual or auditory impairments. Practical examples guide users in implementing accessibility features effectively, aligning with modern standards of inclusivity.

9.6 Troubleshooting Advanced Features

As PowerPoint evolves with new features, users may encounter challenges specific to advanced functionalities. This part of the chapter provides targeted troubleshooting tips for advanced features introduced in earlier chapters, such as SmartArt, 3D models, and macros.

Readers will gain insights into diagnosing issues related to advanced animations, complex charts, and interactive elements. The chapter emphasizes a systematic approach to troubleshooting, empowering users to identify and resolve issues in advanced PowerPoint presentations.

9.7 User Support and Community Resources

When facing challenges, having access to user support and community resources can be invaluable. This section guides users on how to leverage official support channels, community forums, and online resources to seek assistance and solutions for specific issues.

Readers will explore the wealth of knowledge available in online communities, where users share experiences, tips, and solutions. The chapter encourages users to actively participate in these communities, fostering a collaborative environment where knowledge is shared and common issues are addressed collectively.

9.8 Future-Proofing Presentations

As technology evolves, future-proofing presentations becomes a strategic consideration. This concluding part of the chapter explores techniques for creating presentations that are adaptable to future changes in technology and software. From file format considerations to designing presentations with scalability in mind, readers will gain insights into future-proofing their presentations.

The chapter concludes with a reflection on the significance of troubleshooting and optimization as essential skills in the ongoing journey of mastering PowerPoint. Users are encouraged to view challenges as opportunities for growth and learning, positioning themselves to navigate the ever-changing landscape of presentation technology effectively.

CHAPTER TEN

MASTERING POWERPOINT FOR SPECIALIZED USE CASES

As we delve deeper into "Mastering Microsoft PowerPoint 2024," Chapter 10 takes us on a journey into specialized use cases, showcasing how PowerPoint can be tailored to meet unique needs across various domains. From educators to business professionals, this chapter explores advanced features and techniques for specialized applications, providing users with the tools to excel in their specific fields.

10.1 PowerPoint in Education

The chapter kicks off by exploring the extensive applications of PowerPoint in the field of education. Teachers, educators, and instructional designers will discover advanced features for creating engaging and interactive learning materials. Topics include incorporating multimedia elements, creating interactive quizzes, and leveraging animations for educational purposes.

Readers will gain insights into effective ways of structuring educational presentations, creating visual aids for lectures, and utilizing PowerPoint as a platform for e-learning. The chapter emphasizes the role of PowerPoint in facilitating active learning and enhancing the educational experience for both instructors and students.

10.2 PowerPoint for Business Reports and Dashboards

Business professionals often rely on PowerPoint to communicate complex data and insights. This section delves into advanced techniques for creating compelling business reports and dashboards. Users will explore data visualization strategies, linking PowerPoint to external data sources, and creating dynamic dashboards for executive presentations.

The chapter guides business analysts and professionals through the process of designing reports that convey key metrics effectively. Topics include integrating Excel data, using SmartArt for business process illustrations, and incorporating live data feeds for up-to-the-minute reporting.

10.3 PowerPoint for Sales and Marketing Presentations

Sales and marketing professionals can elevate their presentations to new heights with advanced PowerPoint features. This part of the chapter explores techniques for creating persuasive sales pitches, captivating marketing presentations, and impactful product demonstrations. Users will discover strategies for incorporating multimedia, customizing themes to align with branding, and leveraging animations to create compelling narratives.

Practical examples and case studies showcase successful sales and marketing presentations, providing inspiration and guidance for users in these specialized fields. The chapter emphasizes the importance of visual storytelling and audience engagement in sales and marketing contexts.

10.4 PowerPoint in Research and Data Analysis

Researchers and analysts often use PowerPoint to communicate their findings and insights. This section delves into advanced techniques for creating presentations in the realm of research and data analysis. Users will explore data visualization methods, effective storytelling with data, and strategies for presenting complex research findings.

The chapter guides researchers through the process of designing visually compelling slides that convey the significance of their work. Topics include advanced chart customization, incorporating interactive elements for data exploration, and creating presentations that resonate with both academic and non-academic audiences.

10.5 PowerPoint for Nonprofits and Advocacy

Nonprofits and advocacy groups can harness the power of PowerPoint to convey their messages with impact. This part of the chapter explores advanced features for creating presentations that inspire action and support. Users will discover techniques for integrating multimedia, crafting compelling narratives, and leveraging animations to create emotionally resonant presentations.

Practical examples highlight successful nonprofit presentations, showcasing the potential for using PowerPoint as a tool for advocacy and social impact. The chapter emphasizes the role of visual communication in eliciting empathy and driving meaningful change.

10.6 *Accessibility and Inclusivity in Specialized Use Cases*

In all specialized use cases, accessibility and inclusivity are paramount. This section revisits the importance of designing presentations with diverse audiences in mind. Users will explore advanced accessibility features within PowerPoint, ensuring that presentations are inclusive and accessible to individuals with varying abilities.

The chapter provides insights into creating accessible educational materials, business reports, sales presentations, and research findings. Techniques for incorporating alt text, using accessible design principles, and leveraging PowerPoint's accessibility checker are explored in depth.

10.7 Customization and Branding Across Specialized Use Cases

Consistent branding is essential in specialized use cases to maintain a professional and cohesive image. This part of the chapter provides advanced strategies for customizing themes, layouts, and color schemes to align with specific branding guidelines. Users will explore techniques for creating branded templates, ensuring a consistent visual identity across diverse presentations.

Practical examples illustrate the successful implementation of branding in various specialized contexts, from educational materials to business reports and nonprofit presentations. The chapter emphasizes the importance of aligning PowerPoint presentations with organizational branding for a polished and professional appearance.

10.8 Future Trends and Innovations in Specialized Use Cases

As technology evolves, so do the possibilities for specialized use cases in PowerPoint. This concluding section of the chapter explores emerging trends and innovations in specialized applications. From the integration of artificial intelligence to new features tailored for specific industries, readers will gain insights into the future landscape of PowerPoint.

The chapter encourages users to stay informed about evolving trends, experiment with new features, and embrace innovative approaches in their respective fields. By remaining adaptable and forward-thinking, users can position themselves to leverage the latest advancements in PowerPoint for specialized use cases.

CHAPTER ELEVEN

ADVANCED TIPS AND TRICKS FOR POWERPOINT POWER USERS

Chapter 11 of "Mastering Microsoft PowerPoint 2024" is dedicated to power users who seek to push the boundaries of what's possible in PowerPoint. This chapter delves into advanced tips, tricks, and hidden features that can enhance productivity, creativity, and overall mastery of the application.

11.1 Mastering Keyboard Shortcuts and Hotkeys

Efficiency is key for power users, and mastering keyboard shortcuts can significantly speed up workflows. This section provides an in-depth exploration of essential keyboard shortcuts and hotkeys, covering everything from slide navigation to formatting and alignment. Power users will learn how to navigate PowerPoint with lightning speed, streamlining their interactions and boosting overall productivity.

11.2 Advanced Animation Sequences

Building on the basics of animations covered earlier in the guide, this part of the chapter delves into advanced animation sequences. Power users will discover techniques for creating intricate animations, synchronized sequences, and dynamic transitions. The chapter explores the use of motion paths, custom animations, and advanced timing options to bring presentations to life with a level of sophistication that goes beyond the ordinary.

11.3 Custom Slide Shows and Sections

Power users often need to tailor presentations for different audiences or scenarios. This section explores the creation of custom slide shows and sections within PowerPoint. Readers will gain insights into organizing content for specific purposes, creating tailored presentations without duplicating files, and efficiently navigating through extensive slide decks.

11.4 Advanced Data Analysis with Excel Integration

For power users dealing with data-heavy presentations, seamless integration with Microsoft Excel is crucial. This part of the chapter provides advanced techniques for linking and embedding Excel data within PowerPoint. Users will explore dynamic charts, real-time data updates, and advanced Excel features that enhance the presentation of complex data sets.

11.5 Custom Slide Transitions and Morph Effects

Taking slide transitions to the next level, this section explores custom slide transitions and the Morph transition effect. Power users will learn how to create cinematic transitions between slides, incorporating zooms, rotations, and other dynamic effects. The chapter also covers the innovative Morph transition, allowing for seamless animations and transformations between different slide elements.

11.6 Automation with Macros and VBA

While Chapter 7 introduced the basics of macros and VBA, this part of the chapter dives deeper into automation for power users. Readers will explore advanced VBA programming techniques, create complex macros for intricate tasks, and understand how to automate repetitive actions with precision. The chapter empowers power users to customize PowerPoint to fit their specific needs and streamline complex workflows.

11.7 Collaboration Strategies for Power Users

Collaboration is a key aspect of modern workflows, even for power users. This section provides advanced collaboration strategies, covering co-authoring, version control, and efficient communication within PowerPoint. Power users will gain insights into leveraging cloud-based collaboration features and integrating PowerPoint with other Microsoft 365 tools for seamless teamwork.

11.8 Advanced Customization with XML Editing

For users seeking the utmost customization, this part of the chapter introduces advanced customization using XML editing. Power users will explore the XML structure of PowerPoint files, allowing them to fine-tune elements beyond what's available through the standard user interface. The chapter provides cautionary guidance along with practical examples, ensuring that users can confidently experiment with XML editing to achieve highly personalized presentations.

11.9 Integration with Third-Party Tools and Add-ins

Power users often seek to extend PowerPoint's capabilities by integrating third-party tools and add-ins. This section guides users through the process of discovering, installing, and maximizing the potential of third-party tools. From design enhancements to advanced functionalities, power users will learn how to leverage external resources to augment their PowerPoint experience.

11.10 Tips for Delivering Dynamic Presentations

Beyond the creation phase, power users must master the art of delivering dynamic and engaging presentations. This concluding section provides tips for effective delivery, covering techniques for using Presenter View, incorporating live polls, and managing audience interactions. Power users will gain insights into creating a seamless and professional presentation experience from start to finish.